SCOOBY-DOO!™

AND THE PYRAMIDS OF GIZA

THE PHANTOM PHARAOHS

BY MARK WEAKLAND

Consultant: Professor Ethan Watrall
Department of Anthropology
Michigan State University

CAPSTONE PRESS
a capstone imprint

Inside the office of Mystery Incorporated, Fred showed the gang a grainy video on his cell phone.

"We've got a mystery on our hands," said Fred. "Every evening when the sun goes down, three phantom figures swirl among the Pyramids of Giza."

"Phantoms?" gulped Shaggy. "Like, count me out!"

"Re roo!" said Scooby-Doo, nodding in agreement.

Fred frowned. "Whoever they are, they're scaring away the tourists."

"Come on, Shaggy and Scooby," said Velma. "Those tourists need our help."

Daphne brought up a map on her tablet.

The pyramids sit on a plateau in northern Egypt. They're on the west bank of the Nile River, surrounded by the city of Giza.

Egypt, here we come!

A few days later, the gang was crossing the desert on camels.

"Ryramids!" shouted Scooby-Doo.

"They sure look old," said Shaggy.

Velma nodded. "The Giza pyramids were constructed more than 4,500 years ago."

KHUFU →

KHAFRE →

"The pyramids of Khufu, Khafre, and Menkaure were named after the pharaohs who built them," said Daphne.

"It says here that the pharaohs were worshipped like gods, especially after they died," said Fred, reading from his guidebook. "The pharaohs used their pyramids as massive tombs. Inside, they put everything they needed to live in the next world. Archeologists believe Khufu, Khafre, and Menkaure were buried with food, jewelry, clothes, and furniture."

MENKAURE

SCOOBY FACT

Board games were found inside the tomb of King Tutankhamun, another Egyptian pharaoh. Tutankhamun's tomb was discovered in the Valley of the Kings in Egypt in 1922.

Everyone stood in front of the largest pyramid.
"This is the pyramid of Pharaoh Khufu," said Velma.
"It's known as the Great Pyramid. Khufu began
building it around 2550 B.C. It is the oldest and
largest of the three Pyramids of Giza."

"The Great Pyramid was originally 481 feet high," said Daphne, looking up. "Now it's only 451 feet high. Over time people stripped away the smooth stones that covered it."

SCOOBY FACT

The Great Pyramid was the tallest structure in the world, until the Lincoln Cathedral in England surpassed it in 1300.

From the corner of his eye, Scooby
saw something flutter.

ROH NO!

"What is it, Scoob?" asked Shaggy. Scooby pointed at a shadowy figure moving toward the pyramid.

It's a PH-PH-PH-PHANTOM!

It's headed inside the Great Pyramid. After it!

The gang entered the Great Pyramid and scurried along a sloping corridor. Then they climbed through a passageway that led to the center of the pyramid. The shadowy figure was nowhere to be seen.

It got away! OK, gang. Let's look around for clues.

This is the King's Chamber. The burial room.

Velma pointed at the empty stone sarcophagus in the center of the room. "Don't worry, Shaggy. Any mummies that were in there are long gone."

Archeologists have learned a lot about Khufu's pyramid.

It says here the Great Pyramid is one of the most massive structures ever built. Scientists estimate it's made of 2.3 million blocks of stone. Together the blocks weigh 5.75 million tons.

Daphne pointed to a picture in Fred's guidebook. It showed Khufu's pyramid being built. "The stones were cut from nearby quarries and then hauled on wooden sledges," Daphne said. "Workers could have used water to wet the sand in front of the sledges. That would have made the stones easier to pull."

"Right, Daphne," said Fred, nodding. "To build the pyramid, archeologists think workers used a dirt and sand ramp that spiraled around the structure. Workers could have hauled the stone blocks up the ramp with sledges, rollers, ropers, and levers."

Back outside, all was quiet. The gang stood in front of a temple. "What is this place?" asked Shaggy.

"This is the mortuary temple," said Daphne.

Shaggy shivered. "Mortuary? Like, isn't that where they keep dead bodies?"

Daphne shook her head. "No, not in this case. Mortuary temples were religious buildings in ancient Egypt, like churches are today. After the pharaohs died, people worshipped them like gods. These ceremonies took place in the mortuary temples. Inside, priests made offerings to the dead pharaohs."

"The mortuary temples were part of a larger group of buildings," said Fred. "There were also smaller pyramids nearby, called the queen's pyramids. These were for the mummies of the pharaoh's family members."

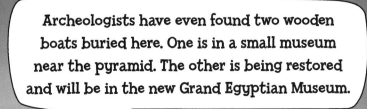

Archeologists have even found two wooden boats buried here. One is in a small museum near the pyramid. The other is being restored and will be in the new Grand Egyptian Museum.

SCOOBY FACT

Archeologists have discovered several long, narrow holes called boat pits near the Great Pyramid. These boat pits are empty now, but they contained more wooden boats for the king.

Like, maybe Pharaoh Khufu thought he could sail into the afterlife.

It's time for us to sail out of here too. We'll come back tomorrow at sunset and see if we can find those phantoms.

The next evening, the gang was back. This time they were looking for clues at the middle pyramid.

"This is the pyramid of Pharaoh Khafre," said Daphne. "Khafre was Khufu's son. He began building his pyramid about 30 years after the Great Pyramid, around 2520 B.C."

"Khafre's pyramid is smaller than Khufu's, but it's still big. It's 707.75 feet long on each side," said Velma. "It was 471 feet high when it was built."

A small figure with a pharaoh's face sprinted past them.

Don't let it get away!

That looks like Pharaoh Khafre!

The gang chased after the figure, but it was gone.

The gang continued their search of the area. "Have archeologists discovered what life was like for the people who built the pyramids?" asked Daphne.

"You bet," said Fred. "Archeologists digging near these pyramids have found shops, homes, and other temples. The ruins of storage areas and bakeries have also been uncovered."

SCOOBY FACT

The pyramids were not constructed by slaves and prisoners. The workers who built the pyramids were treated well and paid.

"Just thinking about bakeries makes me hungry," said Shaggy, holding his rumbling stomach.

Fred continued. "It took thousands of people to build the pyramids. Some archeologists believe as many as 20,000 workers lived near the pyramids. Other people such as bakers, priests, basket weavers, and doctors may have lived there too."

Heading back to their camels, the gang came upon an enormous statue.

"Like, wow!" said Shaggy, looking up at a pair of gigantic paws.

"It's the Sphinx," said Velma. "The statue has a lion's body and a pharaoh's head. Many historians believe the head was modeled after Pharaoh Khafre. The lion's body connected the king to a sun god that the Egyptians worshipped."

Fred shook his head in wonder. "Every one of these monuments shows how powerful the ancient pharaohs were. They had a lot of power over the people in their kingdom."

The gang had one more evening to solve the mystery, and one more pyramid to explore.

"This pyramid was built for Pharaoh Menkaure in 2490 B.C.," said Fred. "It's the smallest of the three pyramids. It's 218 feet high."

"It looks rougher than the others," said Shaggy.

Daphne agreed. "Long ago every Giza pyramid was covered by white, highly polished limestone. Over time the limestone fell off. It was carted away and used to make other buildings."

Rounding a giant stone block, the gang skidded to a halt in front of a souvenir stand. Standing next to a tall man were the three phantoms.

"Hello, I am Mohammad," said the man. He pointed as the three phantoms slowly removed the masks from their faces. "And these are my children."

"The phantom pharaohs are kids!" exclaimed Fred.

"When I heard the tourists talking about phantoms, I had no idea they were my children," said Mohammad.

Tomorrow they will apologize to everyone. Won't you?

Yes, Father.

SCOOBY SNACK-SIZED FACTS

- An Egyptian pharaoh began constructing his pyramid almost as soon as he became king.

- Scientists calculate that it took 20,000 or more workers building continuously for more than 20 years to create the Great Pyramid.

- Some homes and royal palaces were made of mud bricks in ancient Egypt. Most broke down over time. The Pyramids of Giza were made from granite and limestone. They were built to last forever.

- Pharaoh Khafre built his pyramid on the highest spot on the Giza plateau. This makes his pyramid appear taller than the Great Pyramid.

- Ancient Egyptians believed the Nile River's west bank was the land of the dead. Since the pyramids were tombs, they were built west of the river.

GLOSSARY

ancient (AYN-shunt)—from a long time ago

archaeologist (ar-kee-AH-luh-jist)—a scientist who learns about people in the past by digging up old buildings and objects and carefully examining them

chamber (CHAYM-bur)—a large room

corridor (KOR-uh-dor)—a long hallway

granite (GRAN-it)—a hard, gray rock used in the construction of buildings

limestone (LIME-stohn)—a hard rock used in building and to make cement; limestone is formed from the remains of shells and coral

pharaoh (FAIR-oh)—the title of rulers in ancient Egypt

plateau (pla-TOH)—an area of high, flat land

quarry (KWOR-ee)—a place where stone and slate are dug from the ground

sarcophagus (sar-KAH-fuh-guhs)—a stone coffin used by ancient Egyptians

sledge (SLEJ)—a sled placed on runners to carry loads, often pulled by animals

surpass (sur-PASS)—to go beyond

tomb (TOOM)—a grave, room, or building for holding a dead body

READ MORE

Hoobler, Dorothy. *Where Are the Great Pyramids?* Where Is ... ? New York: Grosset & Dunlap, 2015.

Malam, John. *Pyramids.* 100 Facts You Should Know. New York: Gareth Stevens Publishing, 2015.

Stanborough, Rebecca. *The Great Pyramid of Giza.* Engineering Wonders. North Mankato, Minn.: Capstone Press, 2016.

INTERNET SITES

Use FactHound to find Internet sites related to this book.

Visit *www.facthound.com*

Just type in 9781515775133 and go.

Super-cool stuff!

Check out projects, games and lots more at
www.capstonekids.com

INDEX

Published in 2018 by Capstone Press, a Capstone Imprint
1710 Roe Crest Drive
North Mankato, Minnesota 56003
www.mycapstone.com

Library of Congress Cataloging-in-Publication Data
Names: Weakland, Mark, author.
Title: Scooby-Doo! and the pyramids of Giza : the phantom pharaohs / By Mark Weakland.
Description: North Mankato, Minnesota : Capstone Press, 2018. | Series: Scooby-Doo! Unearthing ancient civilizations with Scooby-Doo!
Identifiers: LCCN 2017034028 (print) | LCCN 2017036381 (ebook) | ISBN 9781515775218 (eBook PDF) |
ISBN 9781515775133 (library binding) |
ISBN 9781515775171 (paperback.)
Subjects: LCSH: Pyramids—Egypt—Jizah—Juvenile literature. | Jizah (Egypt)—Antiquities—Juvenile literature. | Egypt—Civilization—332 B.C.–638 A.D.—Juvenile literature. | Ghosts—Egypt—Jizah—Juvenile literature. | Scooby-Doo (Fictitious character)—Juvenile literature.
Classification: LCC DT73.G5 (ebook) | LCC DT73.G5 W43 2018 (print) |
DDC 932/.01—dc23
LC record available at https://lccn.loc.gov/2017034028

Editorial Credits:
Editor: Michelle Hasselius
Designer: Ted Williams
Art Director: Nathan Gassman
Production Specialist: Laura Manthe

Design Elements:
Shutterstock: natashasha

The illustrations in this book were created traditionally, with digital coloring.

TITLES IN THIS SET

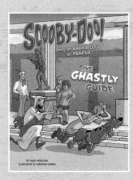